Who's Who
in a
Suburban Community

Jake Miller

Rosen Classroom Books & Materials

New York

Published in 2005 by The Rosen Publishing Group, Inc.
29 East 21st Street, New York, NY 10010

First Edition

Editor: Joanne Randolph
Book Design: Maria E. Melendez
Layout Design: Emily Muschinske

Photo Credits: Cover and title page, © John Henley/CORBIS; p. 5 © Bob Krist/CORBIS; p. 7 © Donna Day/CORBIS; p. 9 © Steve Prezant/CORBIS; p. 11 © Bruce Burkhardt/CORBIS; p. 13 © Rich Meyer/CORBIS; p. 15 © Gaetano/CORBIS; p. 17 © Owen Franken/CORBIS; p. 19 © LWA-Dann Tardif/CORBIS; p. 21 © RNT Productions/CORBIS.

Library of Congress Cataloging-in-Publication Data

Miller, Jake, 1969–
  Who's who in a suburban community / Jake Miller.
      v. cm. — (Communities at work)
  Includes bibliographical references and index.
  Contents: Living in the suburbs — Growing up in a suburban community — Keeping people healthy — What people need — The Police Department — Fighting fires — The local YMCA — Delivering the mail — Eating out — Working together in the suburbs.
  ISBN 1-4042-2789-X (lib. bdg.) — ISBN 1-4042-5032-8 (pbk.)
  1. Suburban life—Juvenile literature. 2. Community life—Juvenile literature. 3. Municipal services—Juvenile literature. [1. Suburban life. 2. Community life. 3. Municipal services.] I. Title. II. Series.

  HT351.M55 2005
  307.74—dc22

                                    2003027871

Manufactured in the United States of America

Contents

Living in the Suburbs   4
Growing Up in the Suburbs   6
Keeping People Healthy   8
What People Need   10
The Police Department   12
Fighting Fires   14
Working at the Local YMCA   16
Delivering the Mail   18
Eating Out   20
Working Together in the Suburbs   22
Glossary   23
Index   24
Web Sites   24

Living in the Suburbs

A **community** is a group of people. A community is also the place where people live, work, and play together. A **suburban** community is a place near a city.

In the suburbs people have more space than people do in a city. They also have more neighbors close by than people do in the country.

Suburban communities are made up of many neighborhoods. Houses are often close together.

Growing Up in the Suburbs

Children in the suburbs live in all different kinds of homes. Some live in houses. Some live in small **apartment** buildings. Some live in **mobile** homes. They all go to school together. They have friends from different places around the community.

This girl and her father stand in front of their house in the suburbs. After school, children may go to an after-school program or to day care. Some children may go home to their parents.

Keeping People Healthy

Doctors, nurses, and dentists are part of the suburban community. They work hard to keep the people in the community healthy.

A **pediatrician** is a doctor who takes care of children. The pediatrician has an office in the community. He or she also works with the local **hospital**. Children who become very sick can get special care there.

A pediatrician cares for a young girl in the hospital. The pediatrician's job is to keep children healthy and to make them feel better if they become sick.

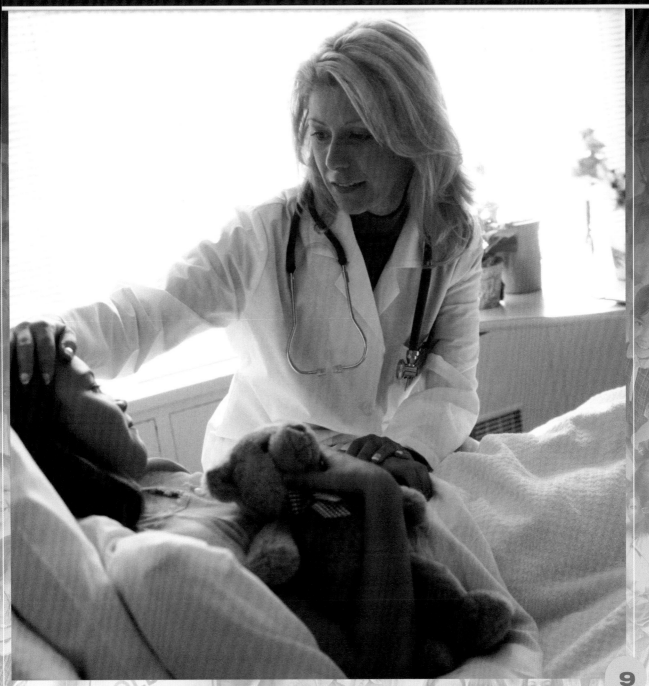

9

What People Need

People in a suburban community need many different **services**. The town takes care of many of these services.

Town workers clean the roads when it snows. They make sure that water pipes bring fresh water to people's homes. People need the water to drink and to cook.

RED OAK ELEMENTARY SCHOOL
SHAKOPEE, MN

A worker fixes a road in a suburban community. People in the suburbs need roads to get to work, the store, or any other place they need to go.

11

The Police Department

Police officers keep the community safe. They move around the community in their police cars. They also move on bicycles and on foot.

Police officers make sure that everyone follows the community's rules. Police officers put people in jail if they hurt other people or take other people's things.

Police officers make sure that people in the community are safe. If someone in a community does not follow the rules, people can get hurt.

Fighting Fires

In some communities being a firefighter is a full-time job. In many suburban communities, **firefighters** are **volunteers**. They have other jobs that they do to earn money.

When there is a fire, the volunteer firefighters stop whatever they are doing. They hurry to the fire station. They work together to put out the fire.

Firefighters work together to fight fires. They keep people, homes, and businesses in their community safe.

Working at the Local YMCA

The YMCA is a suburban community center. Workers at the YMCA offer classes to the people in the community. They teach swimming lessons and art classes.

The workers at the YMCA also make sure that the center is a safe place. The workers at the YMCA are members of the suburban community.

The YMCA is a place in the community where everyone can get together. Here a YMCA worker is teaching a young girl to swim.

Delivering the Mail

Postal workers are an important part of the suburban community. Everyone loves to get a letter or a birthday card in the mail. Important letters and bills also come in the mail.

The people at the post office work to make sure that people in the community receive their mail. They help to keep the suburban community running smoothly.

Some postal workers sort mail. Others sell stamps at the counter. Mail carriers carry the mail to homes and businesses in the community.

Eating Out

COMMUNITY NEWS

Business owners sell things that people in their communities want and need. They also give people jobs, so that people can earn money to buy the things that they want and need.

Business owners are a part of the suburban community, too. The owner of the coffee shop serves food and drinks to many people in the town.

People in the community work at the shop. The server lives in town. He or she walks to work each day. Young adults wash dishes in the kitchen.

People come together at the coffee shop. They meet to share news each week.

Working Together in the Suburbs

People in a suburban community help each other. They buy and sell the **goods** and services they want and need. They work for businesses and for the government. They volunteer at the fire department. They help their neighbors when they have problems. They share good news when they are happy.

Glossary

apartment (uh-PART-ment) Describing a building in which many
people live.

community (kuh-MYOO-nih-tee) A place where people live and
work together, or the people who make up such a place.

firefighters (FYR-fy-ters) Men and women who work to put out fires.

goods (GUDZ) Things that people can buy and sell.

hospital (HOS-pih-tul) A place where doctors work and where
sick people go to become well.

mobile (MOH-bul) Movable.

pediatrician (pee-dee-uh-TRIH-shun) A doctor who treats children.

postal (POH-stul) Having to do with the mail.

services (SIR-vis-ez) Things that people do to or for other people.

suburban (suh-BER-bun) Having to do with an area of homes
and businesses that is near a large city.

volunteers (vah-lun-TEERS) People who work for no money.

Index

A
apartment
    buildings, 6
B
business owners,
    20

F
firefighter(s), 14

G
goods, 22
government, 22

H
hospital, 8

M
mobile homes, 6

N
neighbors, 4, 22

P
pediatrician, 8
police officers, 12
postal workers, 18

S
services, 10, 22
suburbs, 4, 6

T
town workers, 10

V
volunteers, 14

Y
YMCA, 16

Web Sites

Due to the changing nature of Internet links, PowerKids Press has developed an online list of Web sites related to the subject of this book. This site is updated regularly. Please use this link to access the list:

www.powerkidslinks.com/caw/whosuburb/

5012